Everybody's Guide to People Watching

Aaron Wolfgang, Ph.D., C.Psych

REFERENCE

WITHDRAWN FROM
THE LIBRARY

UNIVERSITY OF
WINCHESTER

KA 0332867 8

Everybody's Guide to People Watching

Aaron Wolfgang, Ph.D., C.Psych

INTERCULTURAL PRESS
A Nicholas Brealey Publishing Company

BOSTON • LONDON

UNIVERSITY OF MANCHESTER
LIBRARY

First published by Intercultural Press. For information contact:

Intercultural Press, Inc.
A division of
Nicholas Brealey Publishing
100 City Hall Plaza, Suite 501
Boston, MA 02108 USA
Tel: (+) 617-523-3801
Fax: (+) 617-523-3708
www.interculturalpress.com

Nicholas Brealey Publishing
3-5 Spafield Street
Clerkenwell
London, EC1R 4QB, UK
Tel: (+) 44-207-239-0360
Fax: (+) 44-207-239-0370
www.nicholasbrealey.com

© 1995 by Aaron Wolfgang

All rights reserved. No part of this publication may be repro-
duced in any manner whatsoever without written permis-
sion from the publisher, except in the case of brief quotations
embodied in critical articles or reviews.

Book design and production by Patty J. Topel
Cover design by Lois Leonard Stock

Printed in the United States of America

10 09 08 07 06   5 6 7 8 9

Library of Congress Cataloging–in–Publication Data

Wolfgang, Aaron.
  Everybody's guide to people watching / Aaron Wolfgang.
      p.   cm.
  Includes bibliographical references.
  ISBN 1-877864-36-6
    1. Nonverbal communication (Psychology)   2. Nonver-
bal communication (Psychology)—Cross-cultural studies.
  I. Title.

BF637.N66W65   1995
153.6'9—dc20
                                            95-6156
                                               CIP

For Luba, my wife and friend

UNIVERSITY OF WINCHESTER	
03328678	158.2 / WOL

Table of Contents

Acknowledgments

There were many who assisted and guided me at the different stages in developing and writing this book. In particular, I would like to express my gratitude to my former students Fernando Nunes for his contribution to some chapters on people watching across cultures and Zella Wolofsky for her assistance on the chapter "People Watching on the Job." Also to Mark Thurman, an artist, illustrator, and editor of children's magazines, who made many insightful comments at the early stages regarding the flow of the manuscript. Thanks to my son Kurt for putting in long hours transcribing the material into an orderly computer format. Special thanks to my wife Luba, who kept an encouraging, watchful eye over the grammar and flow during the development of this book.

I would like to acknowledge two people who served as role models and inspirations in writing this guide. They are Edward T. Hall, a social anthropologist, and Desmond Morris, a zoologist and surrealist painter whose books appeal to a wide and diverse audience as well as provide insight into the role of nonverbal behavior in communication in general, and intercultural communication in particular.

Last but not least a special note of thanks to David S. Hoopes, editor in chief, and Toby S. Frank, president of Intercultural Press for their steadfast encouragement and editorial magic to make this a better book.

PART I

Basic Principles

Introduction

People watching is something almost everyone does almost all the time. It has been called the favorite human pastime. As such, it seems simple and obvious: you just observe what is going on around you. In fact, people watching is not quite so simple, especially across cultures, and understanding some of its subtleties can enrich the experience for you.

This book is designed as a guide to increase your knowledge of people watching and to help you to train yourself (and/or others) to be more sensitive observers of other people and their nonverbal behaviors. People watching can be a hobby or, for the traveler who does not speak the languages of the countries or cultures she or he visits, it can be a valuable tool for learning something of the habits and customs of other peoples. (Of course, it is valuable even if you *do* speak the language!) Perhaps people watching will make the way you spend some of your free time more interesting. Who knows? Being a good people watcher might help you land a job or find a mate.

Ideally, through reading this book, you should become more understanding, more accepting, and less critical or fearful of people who are different because of culture or race. I also hope that by people watching on a more conscious level, you can overcome some of the feelings of isolation which result from an ever advancing technological society. Such a society conditions you to be less personal and more tuned in to the electronic gadgetry that increasingly dominates our lives.

Undoubtedly people watching has been going on as long as human beings have inhabited the earth, and it probably had an important survival function for the species. Watching for signals of who is friend or foe must always have been a basic human activity, though people watching may have less urgency now than it did 100,000 years ago. We don't have to be quite as vigilant about others harming us in our everyday lives, though that point might be debated by people who live in or enter areas where there is a great deal of violence or crime. Self-protection is still a function of people watching; but since it is not as critical to our survival as it was originally, we may have become less sensitive and less attentive to or, worse, too easily misread those around us.

People watching is not necessarily a conscious activity. It goes on all the time, unconsciously as well. At this level of awareness we are constantly processing information about what people around us are doing. It is part of the omnipresent background to our lives.

Conscious people watching is special and occurs for many reasons. It has been suggested that we can even become silent friends through people watching. People watching, as one person put it, is like being in touch with friends you never met. This was said by an Irishman living in Canada who likes to sit and smoke his pipe and watch how people use their time. He walks away feeling in touch with others.

In this book I will give special attention to people watching across cultures. People watching at home is fascinating and useful. But people watching across cultures can be particularly interesting and valuable because of the differences in what various kinds of nonverbal behaviors mean from culture to culture. A misperception of the meaning of nonverbal behavior has been shown by communication specialists to be one of the major barriers to effective intercultural communication or cross-cultural understanding. For instance, if a North American was a supervisor in a work situation where someone from Asia (e.g., China) smiled at the supervisor when an error at the job site was made, the American might interpret that behavior as strange and inappropriate. (In the case of a Korean, the more pronounced the error, the more vigorous would be the smile—to reflect sorrow and embarrassment for the error.) A sensitive people watcher would inquire about the meaning of the smile. He or she would discover that it was a way of showing respect and attempting to maintain interpersonal harmony in the situation. People watching, and the effort you make to decipher what you observe, open a special window into a culture which is strange to you and helps you bridge the communication gap.

But you don't have to go to another country to engage in cross-cultural people watching. Even at home, society is increasingly diverse. This is certainly true in the United States and Canada and is true as well in other countries which are experiencing the impact of immigration, the movement of refugees, or simply a rise in tourism and international sojourning. Thus, people watching across cultures is something you are likely to be engaging in at almost any time, even if you never leave your doorstep. You can learn as much at home from this cross-cultural activity as you can abroad.

Finally, this book was written for people of all ages everywhere in the world. After all, people watching starts in every one of us in early infancy and goes on for a lifetime. The things I write about will be based on my personal experience and research, as well as on the personal experiences and observations of others. I wish you all, wherever you live, a happy reading and learning experience.

2

Confessions of a People Watcher

As long as I can remember, I have been a people watcher. What I particularly like to focus on is people's faces. There are a variety of faces as well as facial expressions out there. They seem to come alive most strongly in conversations. Neutral expressions prevail when people are walking silently in public places. But when they greet each other, start to chat, or enter into a serious discussion, their faces become animated and revealing.

How about right here starting to test your skills as a people watcher. The face is an important primary site for revealing our emotions, attitudes, and feelings. It is, in fact, one of the oldest and most intensely studied channels of communication. What I want you to do is look carefully at each of the forty faces pictured on the next pages. Then, in the parentheses under each face write the letter code for the facial expression, choosing from the seven listed below the one which best describes the expression on each of them.

Interest–I	**Happiness–H**	**Surprise–SU**
Sadness–SA	**Anger–A**	**Neutral–N**
	Contempt–C	

Here are four samples:

A ( )   B ( )   C ( )   D ( )

The answers are A=Happy, B=Happy, C=Interest, D=Interest

Wolfgang Interracial Face Expression Test

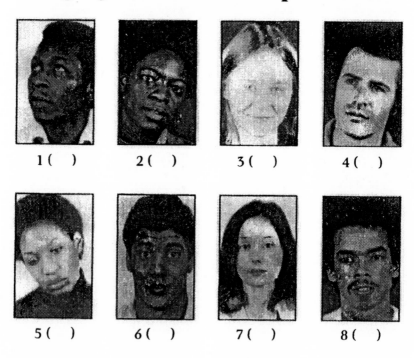

1 ( )   2 ( )   3 ( )   4 ( )

5 ( )   6 ( )   7 ( )   8 ( )

Interest–I, Happiness–H, Surprise–SU, Sadness–SA, Anger–A, Neutral–N, Contempt–C

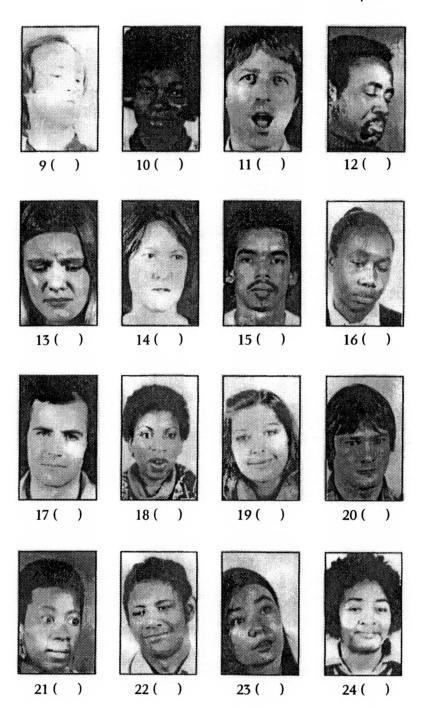

9 (   )   10 (   )   11 (   )   12 (   )

13 (   )   14 (   )   15 (   )   16 (   )

17 (   )   18 (   )   19 (   )   20 (   )

21 (   )   22 (   )   23 (   )   24 (   )

Interest-I, Happiness-H, Surprise-SU, Sadness-SA, Anger-A, Neutral-N, Contempt-C

25 (   )   26 (   )   27 (   )   28 (   )

29 (   )   30 (   )   31 (   )   32 (   )

33 (   )   34 (   )   35 (   )   36 (   )

37 (   )   38 (   )   39 (   )   40 (   )

Interest–I, Happiness–H, Surprise–SU, Sadness–SA, Anger–A, Neutral–N, Contempt–C

Answers:

1.	I	11.	SU	21.	SU	31.	C
2.	N	12.	C	22.	H	32.	SA
3.	H	13.	SA	23.	I	33.	C
4.	I	14.	A	24.	H	34.	N
5.	SA	15.	N	25.	A	35.	SA
6.	SU	16.	SA	26.	N	36.	H
7.	N	17.	N	27.	SU	37.	SU
8.	A	18.	SU	28.	H	38.	A
9.	C	19.	H	29.	I	39.	N
10.	H	20.	A	30.	H	40.	A

The West Indian expressions are numbers:

1, 2, 5, 6, 8, 10, 12, 15, 16, 18, 21, 22, 24, 25, 29, 31, 34, 36, 38, 39

The white Anglo-Saxon expressions are numbers:

3, 4, 7, 9, 11, 13, 14, 17, 19, 20, 23, 26, 27, 28, 30, 32, 33, 35, 37, 40

The male faces are numbers:

1, 4, 6, 8, 9, 11, 12, 15, 17, 20, 22, 25, 28, 30, 32, 34, 36, 37, 39, 40

The female faces are numbers:

2, 3, 5, 7, 10, 13, 14, 16, 18, 19, 21, 23, 24, 26, 27, 29, 31, 33, 35, 38

How well did you do overall? When comparing yourself to others who have taken this quiz, 28 correct is good, 30 correct is very good, and 32 correct out of 40 is excellent. If you wish, see how well you did on West Indian facial expressions compared to white Anglo-Saxon expressions, or how well you did on male faces compared to female. See which emotions you had difficulty recognizing.

As an exercise, next time you are in a social situation, find one or more people to watch. What are their facial expressions telling you? Happiness? Interest? Surprise? How do the expressions on the face quiz match the ones you observe in various social situations? You also might want to observe your own facial expressions. How aware are you of the ones you most commonly use? Start taking note of them. Mimic the facial expressions on the quiz in front of a mirror. In what situations do you find yourself showing a happy, sad, neutral, or an angry face? How do people react to you when you show these faces? What would happen if, for a whole day, you showed everyone your happy face or sad face? How would you expect people to react to you?

When I'm out walking, sitting in a café, or at the airport, I sometimes try to engage people's eyes for a moment. Eye contact can be a surprisingly intense experience between strangers. Sometimes people will meet my eyes for a second, smile slightly, and look away. Others will give me a blank stare. Still others will avoid my eyes and hurry on their way. Eyes tend to open onto the inner self, and if you stare too long people may become defensive or embarrassed. Once in Canada a punk rocker tried to spit on me when I was looking intently at him on the street. "What's the matter," he said belligerently, "do I have egg on my face?" At Club Med I found myself looking intently at a French woman who was not particularly physically attractive but who had a very interesting face. After some minutes of appearing quite uncomfortable, she approached me and asked if I would stop. "You make me feel very self-conscious," she said.

I also find intriguing how people communicate by *touching*. Perhaps this is so because I come from a culture that is not touch oriented. Around the world I've watched people in public places like markets, zoos, subways, airports, and cafés to see how they communicate through touch. I was particularly interested when I found touching behavior different from what I was used to in North America. In Cairo, for instance, there were two young men walking in the zoo with their baby fingers interlocked, and in Israel women leisurely strolled in the marketplaces or sauntered through the streets of Tel Aviv arm-in-arm or arm-on-shoulder. In Canada and the United States these behaviors are seen infrequently and then may precipitate second looks.

Men and women, of course, express themselves to one another through touch. Consider the different ways you've seen them make physical contact in public—from touching fingers to putting hands in each other's pockets to lying on the grass in a park kissing.

One thing I find particularly interesting is how people *mir-*

ror or imitate each other's nonverbal behavior without realizing it. They seem to be especially in tune with each other. In London I saw two bobbies in Hyde Park walking together, at the same pace, with their arms crossed behind their backs. They seemed like duplicates of each other in looks and in movement. In the Luxembourg Gardens of Paris I chuckled to myself when I saw two people licking their ice cream cones in unison. Sometimes taking on the body posture or facial expression of another gives me an idea of how that person is feeling at the moment. I like watching groups of people engaged in synchronous activities such as laughing or clapping, because it makes me aware that there is much harmony among people in the world despite so much evident disharmony.

It is also interesting to watch how people *greet* each other when they meet. Here, too, we can see a kind of synchrony. Latins and Arabs hug and kiss each other on the cheek; others shake hands, smile, and embrace. There is nothing like the bear hug of a Russian–born friend to knock the breath out of you.

One of the most enjoyable instances of synchrony I have ever experienced was when my granddaughter Chloe tried to mimic my smiling face and laughing voice when she was eight months old.

3

Why People People Watch

Let's start by inviting you to answer some questions about why you people watch and then compare those answers with what others say about *their* reasons for people watching. This questionnaire was used as part of the interviews of over ninety people conducted by me and my graduate assistants during the preparation of this book. It was administered to men and women of different social and cultural backgrounds. See how you respond.

1. Do you engage in people watching? Can you describe what you do when you are people watching?

2. Why do you people watch?

3. Where do you like to people watch?

4. How do you people watch?

5. Do people notice you watching them?

6. What do you focus on when you are people watching?

7. What do you find rewarding about people watching?

8. Do you have any favorite places where you watch?

9. Have you noticed anything obnoxious or vulgar that people do while you are watching?

10. Has people watching helped you in your job?

11. How do you feel about people watching you?

Now read back over your answers. Did you learn anything new about your people-watching habits? How do you think your friends or persons close to you would answer the questions? Here are some highlights and the most frequently given answers from the ninety interviewees. How are they similar to or different from yours?

1. Do you engage in people watching? Can you describe what you do when you are people watching?

   Almost all the respondents said yes (98 percent), they do people watch. Twice as many males said they try to analyze people when watching compared to females, who are more inclined to try to size up people, to tell what they are like from their clothes, or to make up scenarios about them. Other more common answers were "I glance when watching" or "it just happens naturally."

2. Why do you people watch?

   "It's interesting," "satisfies my curiosity," "to analyze people."

3. Where do you like to people watch?

   "Anywhere and everywhere," "in the workplace."

4. How do you people watch?

   "Casual glances," "it's like breathing," "it's natural."

5. Do people notice you watching them?

   "Sometimes," "never"; a few said things like "hope not," and "I avert my eyes."

6. What do you focus on when you are people watching?

   Females focus more on clothes and the face when watching. Body language in general or movement was most frequently mentioned as a focal point by males.

7. What do you find rewarding about people watching?

   "Entertaining," "fun," "a variety of people to watch." Three times as many males as females said they can learn something from people watching.

8. Do you have any favorite places where you watch?

   "No place," "any place."

9. Have you noticed anything obnoxious or vulgar that people do while you are watching?

   Unpleasant personal hygiene (e.g., "spitting," "picking nose"); inconsiderate or selfish behavior (e.g., using ghetto blasters, arguing).

10. Has people watching helped you in your job?

    Over 76 percent of the people answered yes to this question. Some ways people watching has helped on the job were: "makes you more aware of whether a customer is impressed with your product," "can tell by the lost look on people's faces if they need help in the library," "can tell how to approach a client by watching body language," "can see what mood they are in."

11. How do you feel about people watching you?

    More females than males felt uncomfortable or self-conscious about people watching them. Of the total responses, 32 percent of the men felt comfortable about being watched and 19 percent of the women.

There were some interesting contrasts between male and female respondents relative to what each focused on, the rewards of people watching, and the comfort level in oneself being watched.

Here is a sample interview with a forty-one-year-old woman whose responses gave food for thought. She said at the start of the interview that people watching was her favorite pastime. She remarked that she likes people and noted that she watched them because it connected her with others. She also loved to make up stories about the people she was watching, which was a relatively common response among the interviewees. Below are her answers to the people-watching questions. How do you compare yourself to her?

1. Do you engage in people watching? Can you describe what you do when you are people watching?

   I look at faces first, quickly run down the body, go back to the eyes...look for kindness, sadness. I feel the vibes of the person; then I watch interactions with others.

2. Why do you people watch?

   To learn about others, to connect with others, to study our wonderful species.

3. Where do you like to people watch?

   In parks, at concerts, everywhere.

4. How do you people watch? Do people notice you watching them?

   They are not aware of me watching them. I watch them guardedly.

5. What do you focus on when you are people watching?

   Faces, eyes, jewelry. I like to construct a story based on that.

6. What do you find rewarding about people watching?

   What does anyone find rewarding about an addiction?

7. Do you watch people who are alone or who are in conversation?

   Both.

8. Have you noticed anything that people do when you are people watching that you find obnoxious or vulgar?

   Men leering at women.

9. Has people watching helped you in your job?

   For sure.

By tuning in to the people-watching approaches of others as well as your own, you become more focused and aware. As the woman said about people watching: "You never feel alone and it can help you feel connected to others."

Why do people people watch? There seem to be a couple of basic reasons. First, because it is fun and keeps them from getting bored. Think of the times you have been stuck somewhere you didn't want to be and entertained yourself by watching what people were doing. It's satisfying, many of our respondents said, or, simply, it's amusing.

The second most popular reason is that you can learn from it, particularly in watching people you admire so that you can incorporate their behaviors into your own behavior patterns. Self-improvement or understanding the opposite sex or learning how to communicate better in work and social situations, no matter how simple, are compelling reasons for people watching.

As a result of people watching—especially since 1985, when I first began collecting material for this book—I've become much more conscious of and focused on working out my feelings, understanding how others respond to the world around them, and getting a better sense of how they respond to me in particular.

Through people watching, I've become more aware of how I present myself and how I might affect other people. This awareness has penetrated my personal relationships and my teaching and has influenced my travels. I also feel I've developed a deeper sensitivity to people by being more aware of how others respond to me and how I relate to them. Not only do I watch others and how they project their moods, attitudes, and feelings, but I also watch myself for the same reasons. I try to focus on what I say and, more importantly, on what my nonverbal behavior is saying to others in a conversation. In addition, I feel I've become a better listener, and I try not to put others off by my nonverbal behavior.

People watching has been of great benefit to me in my travels around the world. For one thing, I never feel lonely when traveling by myself. For another, observing different kinds of nonverbal behavior makes me realize that what's accepted in my culture may not be in another. I remember when I was doing some filming in a marketplace in Palermo, a group of men motioned to my crew with their arms extended, palms down and fingers moving back and forth. We thought it meant "go away." As we prepared to leave, one of the men came forward, smiled, and taking our arms invited us for some wine. We found out later that the gesture meant "come here."

When I asked others if they engaged in people watching while traveling, almost everyone said yes. A novelist and poet from Scotland said that she loved being an observer, a passive spectator absorbing sensations of other people which she subsequently translated into her prose and poetry.

Being a sensitive people watcher has helped me out of potentially dangerous situations. In Rio de Janeiro, when a group of men, dressed up as women on New Year's Eve, asked me to take their pictures, I made a gesture with thumb and forefinger that in the United States means A–OK. Their faces immediately changed from smiling friendliness to anger and puzzlement. I quickly caught their response and switched to the thumbs-up gesture—which is apparently more universal than the other. They smiled and I took their pictures. I later found out that in Brazil the circled configuration of finger and thumb we interpret as A–OK means something rude and obscene.

While in the Bahamas, my companion and I were window shopping one evening in the bazaar. Suddenly, a group of angry Bahamian men came toward us protesting that the casinos were run only by whites and that only whites were hired for good jobs. Watching carefully, I deduced that the one doing most of the talking was their leader. I displayed my best listening skills. As much as I felt threatened by their aggressive behavior, I reined in my fear and extended my hand. The leader took it, gave it a strong shake, and said, "You're OK." Then the group left. My people-watching skills had paid off. We kept calm and listened patiently. Our non-verbal behavior reflected our respect for them and our sympathy for their position. Think back. Can you remember situations in which effective nonverbal behavior has helped you respond appropriately when words were inadequate?

My two people-watching research assistants, Heather and Zella, who interviewed scores of people for this project, were strongly affected by the experience. Heather said that she now feels freer to watch others without her former reserve. She is also not as self-conscious when others watch her, because she now realizes that it is simply human beings doing something irrepressibly fascinating. She sees people watching as part of "a life process that takes us all down the path of learning and awakening."

Zella found that she became more focused in her people watching. She told about waiting in her car at a traffic light and staring at people crossing the street. She said she was watching one small second of their lives and wanted to know more about each of them. She asked herself where they were going, were they married, were they meeting friends, what they did at work. "I found myself falling in love with people. People watching has an addictive quality to it." A new vista had opened for her, and she began to become more aware of the complexity of people's interactions (mothers and children, husbands and wives, etc.). She said that by learning to people watch more consciously, she found that nobody was ugly and that beautiful people were "gifts to look at." She became more tuned in to the "deep common thread that binds us all together."

The experience of Heather and Zella makes it clear that by developing a greater consciousness of your people-watching proclivities you become more comfortable around strangers, more aware of the things that make human beings similar and/or different, more capable of getting close to other people. And it is an experience easily available to all of us.

A painter once told me that he watches the way people dress and move and look. From that, he tries to identify them or give them an apt description, such as middle class, working class, sexy, uptight, confident, rich, poor, radical, or conformist. He then translates these into feelings that enable him to paint his subjects more intuitively.

Some people watchers imagine what other people's lives are like out of a sense of connectedness. A thirty-seven-year-old writer from Toronto said she felt that people watching was a necessity and that people were more intriguing subjects than landscapes, which were great for watching too. But people watching was more exciting and helped her write about people more realistically.

People watching can be valuable in almost any human context. Take competitive sports. In tennis, I find that my game improves significantly when I focus on what my opponent is doing, not only in the game but during the warm-up as well. I observe the shots my opponent goes for, I look for indications of his or her endurance level, and I note how angry or emotional he or she acts after making an error. All these have a significant effect on how I will play the game. I also try to throw my opponent off through my nonverbal behavior. When coming for a net shot, I orient my body one way and hit the ball in the other direction.

People Watching on the Job

Simply being able to observe the dress codes of different work environments is useful. Each workplace has its own code of dress and its own set of behaviors as well as its own culture. Learning that culture is critical to being able to function effectively on the job. Seminars are given on an organization's culture to help people understand and adapt to it. The alert people watcher has the advantage of being able to pick up quickly and easily large amounts of information about a new organizational environment just through careful observation.

One of the most important components of getting a job is having a successful job interview. Being a sensitive people watcher and processing more incoming information at a conscious level than we normally do enables us to use that information more appropriately and effectively. As an example, imagine yourself walking into an office for a job interview. Picture a receptionist who is warm and friendly. How do you feel about the company? About yourself? Now picture a receptionist who is cold and aloof. What impressions have you gotten about the company? How are you feeling about yourself?

Just as you are observing the people in your environment, they too may be watching you. The receptionist is almost certainly taking in information and evaluating your appropriateness for the job. In fact, a business executive once said that as he ushered prospective employees into his office, he would look back to his receptionist for a thumbs-up or a thumbs-down sign. Although the final decision of an employment offer was not totally made on this basis, this particular executive placed a great deal of confidence in his receptionist's people-watching abilities. First impressions are important. Indeed, researchers tell us that most decisions about an applicant are made in the first few minutes of the interview, with the rest of the time spent collecting information and impressions designed to prove the correctness of the decision. Sometimes the decision is made in the first few *seconds* of contact.

Once you're in the interview room, your people-watching skills can guide you through the rapids of dangerous visual and other nonverbal cues, the failure to spot or the misinterpretation of which can quickly crush your employment hopes. See what cues you pick up from these two possible scenarios.

First scenario. The interviewer comes to the door, extends her hand, makes eye contact, and greets you with a warm smile. If you're smart you will have insured that your coat and other belongings are held in your left arm in order to free your right hand for the initial handshake. She then indicates by a gesture where you should sit and engages in some chitchat. What have you noticed about the interviewer so far, and how has this affected your feelings as you are beginning this interview?

Second scenario. The receptionist tells you that you may now go into the office. As you enter, the interviewer is sitting behind the desk, reading. She does not look up to greet you or acknowledge that you are there. What does this say about the interviewer and/or your chances for the job? Will you take a different tack than you would in the other interview? Or, what assumptions will you make about the interviewer, the company, and the desirability of the job?

Throughout the interview the observant people watcher will notice subtle facial expressions and body posture which give clues as to the course of the interview. If you observe that the interviewer has begun to allow her eyes to wander, you can probably guess that she is distracted or not listening to you. What might you do? Respond more succinctly? Increase the volume of your voice? Vary your tone? Shift your position?

Perhaps you've struck it lucky. Have you both sat forward in your seats? Have you relaxed simultaneously? Have you smiled at the same time? This could actually be a graceful ballet of human interaction, the kind of synchrony we discussed earlier. Watch for this in an interview. If it occurs, it is almost certain the interview is going well.

An observant people watcher will be able to sense discomfort in the interviewer and may be able to clarify points of confusion. A frown or a moment of hesitancy by the interviewer may indicate a negative response. The sensitive people watcher will also catch signs of impatience or distraction and will give answers which are shorter and to the point.

One unsuccessful job seeker came to me for advice. When I asked about how he behaved in the interviews, he said that interviews annoyed him and that he took the lead, offering his hand first and controlling the discussion because he didn't want to feel in the interviewer's power. I suggested he let the interviewer take the lead—after all "you're the guest in his or her territory." When next I saw him he said he'd followed my advice and had gotten an offer of a job, unfortunately one he didn't want!

An interviewer may not always be skilled in conducting interviews and may not know how to bring the interview to a graceful ending. An observant people watcher will be able to sense when this is happening by watching for hesitation, a change in the tempo of questions, or a repetition of subject matter. When this is observed, the sensitive people watcher can take some control and end the interview gracefully.

On the job, people in sales, teaching, counseling, health care, and police work (to name a few) can certainly benefit from people watching. The salesperson needs to be a sensitive people watcher to assess whether the customer is ready to buy or is merely interested in gathering information about the product. Teachers and counselors benefit by picking up signals indicating a readiness to communicate or learn. In health care, workers can identify clues reflecting the physical and emotional state of their patients. My son-in-law Peter, a police officer working in a high-crime area of Los Angeles, told me that he needs to be a keen people watcher to do his work properly. He says, for instance, that he can tell from people watching if people are on drugs and what kinds of drugs they are using.

An airline pilot we interviewed said people watching gave him a better sense of his passengers being real people, which made him feel more personal responsibility toward them in his job. A bus driver said that people watching helped him treat other people better. By watching people interact, he became more conscious of the importance of people treating each other as they wished themselves to be treated.

Supervisory and management personnel from a variety of occupations related time and again how their people-watching skills gave them better insight into their employees and helped them "read" what people were trying to say to them nonverbally.

Other professionals used people watching in their work. A trial lawyer felt that he could read the opposing lawyer's reactions better because of people watching. He concentrated on their faces and observed how his arguments were affecting the other lawyers, which gave him clues as to how to deal with witnesses.

Recreation therapists working with the physically disabled at a medical center also watched faces, because their patients were confined to wheelchairs or beds and were sometimes paralyzed from the neck down. Communication via body language was therefore restricted. One such therapist who worked with severely handicapped children said that often her patients' faces were the only indication she had of their feelings and moods.

5

People Watching and Nonverbal Behavior

Central to the whole idea of people watching—and therefore to becoming more aware of it and increasing your skills—is the concept of nonverbal communication or nonverbal behavior. In addition to teaching courses and researching the subject for many years, I have organized international conferences around it, produced a film and edited two books on the subject, and developed for a variety of uses the tests which appear in this book.

What is nonverbal behavior and what role does it play in people watching? In its most basic definition, it is behavior that transcends the spoken word, that adds to and enhances what we say to each other. Nonverbal communication frequently carries more of the message we are trying to communicate than the words we speak. Indeed, some communication specialists believe that nonverbal behavior can carry as much as 80 percent of the meaning we are trying to communicate verbally.

There are two aspects of nonverbal behavior that play a particularly important role in communication. One is called *kinesics*, a word coined by anthropologist Ray Birdwhistell, which refers to patterns of body movement, popularly known as body language. Kinesics includes such behaviors as facial expressions, eye contact, hand gestures, posture, head move-

UNIVERSITY OF WINCHESTER
LIBRARY

ment, and the way we walk. Body language tells us a lot about how people feel about themselves and about others with whom they are interacting. For instance, if Canadians or Americans like another person, the probability is greater that they will make more eye contact, smile more, give more affirmative head nods, and lean more toward that person in conversation than to someone in whom they have little interest. In the case of people we actively dislike, we may avoid looking the person in the eye entirely or perhaps engage in intense, aggressive, or even belligerent eye contact. We will certainly smile less, if at all, and give few affirming nods. In addition, our bodies and/or facial muscles are likely to tense up. We will probably also stand farther apart from them than we do from people to whom we wish to communicate friendliness—which brings us to *proxemics.*

Proxemics is the word first used by anthropologist Edward T. Hall to identify the manner in which people use space in relation to one another (and which he discusses in his excellent study *The Hidden Dimension).* The distance people stand from each other and the kind of space they seem to prefer in social situations (do they like to be in groups where people jostle each other or do they tend to pull away and want to be more physically separate?) determine how they behave in crowded areas, e.g., elevators, subways, and outdoor markets. People, according to some anthropologists and psychologists, exist in envelopes of private space beginning in most cultures at or some inches from the body and into which only others with whom the person is intimate are allowed. It is interesting to watch how people manage that private space when dealing with each other in public.

It is important to note here that customs in body language and the use of space vary significantly from culture to culture. Mexicans and other Latin Americans, for instance, stand closer when engaging in everyday social conversation than do the Japanese or North Americans. The meaning of gestures, such as the A–OK thumb and finger circle I used in Brazil, can have significantly different meanings in different cultures (see Desmond Morris's valuable comparative study *Gestures).* In Part II we will discuss in more detail the significance of cultural differences in people watching.

Nonverbal behavior is central to people watching. It is not only what people say but how they look and act while saying it that is important in trying to understand the full meaning of a conversation. In most people watching, you can't hear the conversation anyway. But an understanding of nonverbal communication is also a special tool. By focusing on, understanding, and being able to interpret nonverbal behavior, we have the opportunity to observe and assess the complex process of human conversation and interaction almost as if we were invisible participants. Not being able to hear the verbal exchange is, in a way, an advantage, since in nonverbal behavior we are watching something more authentic and spontaneous than verbal behavior, particularly when it concerns our emotions and feelings. It is difficult for people to rehearse what hand gestures they will use, what distance they will keep from others, and what facial expression they will show when conversing with another person. These are unconscious behaviors that often reveal people's reactions to each other more accurately than words.

Many psychologists think that since nonverbal behavior operates primarily at the unconscious level, outside of awareness, it can be trusted more than words. It is also thought that nonverbal behavior is more primitive, that it transmits feelings, emotions, and attitudes at a more visceral level. Words, of course, play an important role in conveying ideas and factual information, but lack vitality and would appear mechanical or empty without some form of accompanying nonverbal expression. Looking at the issue from this perspective—that nonverbal behavior (1) goes on all the time and (2) is critical to the communication process—then one is forced to conclude that it is impossible to *not* communicate. In other words, we communicate and reveal things about ourselves all the time through body language whether or not anything is coming out of our mouths. Even when there are no words spoken, we continuously reveal things about ourselves through nonverbal behavior. The body, the face, the eyes are always speaking. Nonverbal behavior is a silent but powerful language.

The Process of
People Watching

What are the most effective or satisfying ways of listening to people's silent language, which is at the heart of the people-watching experience? That, of course, depends principally on you and on how involved you want to be with the people you are watching. You can be a casual observer or spectator if you wish, though the closer you come to the people you watch, the more your senses come into play and the richer and more complex the experience is. The latter calls for exercising more social and communication skills of your own. (We'll give this subject a closer look later in the book when we discuss the social skills embodied in the acronym SOFT-NESS.) Thus, people watching while sitting in the park on a warm day may involve no more than your visual sense—and your imagination! In a crowded bar, hearing, smell, and even touch are going to be engaged.

Of course, people watching is even accessible to the recluse and in ways that are almost entirely passive. As we know, photographs of people can be almost as revealing as seeing them in real life. And what are movies and television if not prime people-watching activities? At the other extreme is the person who behaves provocatively just to see how others will respond—so they can be "watched." At a party one evening I decided to observe how people reacted when I subtly moved closer and closer to them while we were conversing. Not surprisingly, most of them retreated when their personal space was being invaded. On another occasion I was invited by a TV program to be a consultant for a story they were doing on body language. This involved not only commentary on the subject but walking along a downtown street lightly touching people on the shoulder as I asked for directions. The almost universal response was an abrupt moving away and an avoidance of eye contact. I was violating a cultural norm—strangers don't touch—and the reaction was one of discomfort if not annoyance. And, indeed, I found *myself* uncomfortable deliberately violating those norms, even though I did it for what seemed legitimate purposes.

One question that frequently comes up among people who take their people watching seriously is whether to try to make a record for later use or recall. There are, in our electronic age, a variety of ways this can be done: in video, audio, or traditional photos. These call for special effort to catch the pose or conversation you want and involve a high degree of risk of offending the people being watched.

You can also take notes or dictate your thoughts into a microcassette recorder. You may want to make some notation about the setting or, at a deeper level, identify the categories of emotion you have observed (happiness, sadness, disgust, surprise, interest, anger, etc.). You might want to record which behaviors you see most or least frequently–which in a particular situation, which in men, women, or children, etc.

Taking notes also has its risks in possibly giving offense (unobtrusiveness is the key here), but there are other risks as well. One day at a train station I was carefully but blissfully taking notes on the waiting behavior of the passengers (or potential passengers) there—unaware that (as I later learned from one of my graduate students) two police officers had been people watching *me*—who to them must have looked like a decidedly suspicious character.

Here's a checklist that will get you started:

Facial expressions

Touch

Location of touch

Gaze

Hand gestures

Posture

Posture mirroring

Interpersonal distance

Body orientation (direction facing)

Speech (volume, speed)

And here are a couple of sample notations:

Touched on upper arm frequently during conversation

Steady *eye contact;* enjoyed each other's company

Man *gazing* off in distance; more interested in thought than in the woman with him, or just distracted

Woman striving for *eye contact,* failing, *unhappy* expression, not getting through

You might want to concentrate on a limited number of behaviors at first: touch, for instance, noting how *frequently* the people you observe touch each other, *where* they touch, and *how long* they touch while in conversation or greeting.

You might also ask yourself: Is that a person I would like to know, work with, have as a friend, or marry? What nonverbal signals does this person give off that get my attention? Is it the way she or he smiles, looks, speaks, or stands?

If you want to go a little deeper into the process, here is a way to interpret what you observe and then test your interpretation. There are three steps:

1. Look for or imagine a situation in which you have an opportunity to develop an interpretation of what is going on, e.g., I think these two people work for the same company, are on a sales trip together, and are discussing nonbusiness aspects of the trip.

2. Examine the available clues, then take note of the ones that influenced your interpretation most, e.g., they are dressed in business suits, they are quite familiar with each other, they have Lions Club buttons on their lapels, one is reading a magazine called *Boston* (the destination of the flight they seem to be waiting for), and conversing and laughing quite casually.

3. Verify your interpretation, drawing closer in order to observe and/or hear more. If you are lucky you might encounter someone who can tell you more about them.

When the nonverbal signals are powerful enough for you to make an obvious inference (e.g., a couple you observed holding hands and looking into each other's eyes), clearly no verification is necessary. Oftentimes, however, nonverbal signals are subtle and/or not strong enough (as in the case of the salespersons above) to be conclusive. If in those cases you can verify your interpretation, you will enhance your people-watching skills substantially. Of course, if you simply want to trust your intuition about the people you observe, that is perfectly fine. It depends on your goals in people watching.

One very strong reason for taking care when, how, and if you attempt to keep a record of your people watching is the importance of not disturbing the flow of things. You want people to be natural and spontaneous. This makes it desirable for you to try to blend into the environment. At a children's playground, you might bring a child with you; at an athletic event, wear casual clothes; at a party, mingle. Be careful how much you stare. In certain situations, such as in the subway or elevator, people can be intimidated or become belligerent if you stare at them. Brief casual glances are more appropriate and will be more productive—though there are people, sometimes exhibitionists, who invite stares—unless of course you are interested in seeing what reactions you get when you are staring. One woman told me that she purposely wears a loud, colorful scarf to provoke people to look at her and make comments. Sometimes it is difficult not to stare at people when they stand out.

Actually, a significant number of people (40 percent of those we surveyed in our research) feel flattered, comfortable, or unconcerned about people watching them. Others (30 percent in our survey) feel quite *un*comfortable or self-conscious. Still others said it depended on *who* was watching (8 percent), *why* they were watching (12 percent), and/or *how* they were watching (7 percent).

In the end, people's reactions are a mixed bag, so you will have to feel (or watch!) your way along. Actually it is not difficult to tell if people are feeling uncomfortable or self-conscious about your watching them. They are likely to look away quickly or avoid or lessen eye contact. Their hands may become a little jittery and they might stop smiling.

I must confess, I enjoy people watching most when the people I'm observing seem happy. The reason, put very simply, is that if you observe people smiling, you may end up feeling better and smiling yourself. I've salvaged many a down day by watching people enjoying themselves. Actually, this idea is not so simple as it sounds. Norman Cousins, in his book *Anatomy of an Illness*, has demonstrated quite convincingly that enjoyment can have a pronounced beneficial and healthful effect on sick as well as healthy people. When I'm down I like to go to ice cream parlors and watch people enjoying their ice cream. The zoo has the same effect when I see people having fun watching the monkeys bare their teeth, swing by their tails, and cuddle their young.

At the heart of people watching are the three primary ingredients of every social situation: people, places, and behavior.

All kinds of people engage in social interchange, of course, with different physical features, dress, personalities, body language, etc. Sometimes, at first glance, you may not see the differences. A group of businesspeople may all seem to be wearing the same gray suits (including women) or teenagers the same jeans and T-shirts, but the differences soon—often dramatically—become apparent. I will not even attempt to catalogue these differences or comment individually on them. You already have your own special criteria for observing and categorizing people. The one caution I would make, however, is: take care not to stereotype. Everyone has unique qualities, and that uniqueness will emerge if given a little time and space. More on stereotyping in Part II.

7

Places for People Watching

I *will* comment a little more extensively on some of the choicest *places* for people watching. Outdoor markets are one. Market vendors are often flamboyant or at least very expansive and persistent in selling their goods. They can also be irritable. A vendor at a market in Greece became annoyed when I picked up a tomato to feel it before buying. He abruptly grabbed it out of my hand and shouted something in Greek. Though I didn't understand what he said, I certainly got the message. Now when I go to markets I always watch to see who is feeling the fruit and how the vendors are reacting. Vendors can be persuasive, too. They, of course, want you to believe you are getting the best of everything you buy from them—and want you to buy everything they have to sell you. At a market in Toronto, a vendor once convinced me to buy not only the muffins that I wanted but also cheese, sweets, and bagels I didn't need. He convinced me that all of the things I eventually took home were not only great bargains but delicacies that should not be missed. His personable tone of voice, direct eye contact, and the way he held out his products to me as if they were made of gold were persuasive nonverbal behaviors. The vendor gave the same pitch to others and succeeded every time—or at least so it appeared—in selling customers more than what they came for.

Subways, train stations, and airports are good locations for people watching. People in these places are in transit. Their normal routines are broken. There is an air of uncertainty and indefiniteness about the setting. It is a good environment in which to watch a group of strangers, taskless and in a somewhat unfocused state of mind, negotiating how they are going to relate or not relate to each other. I enjoy watching how they try to protect their personal space. Some will sprawl out or place their bags or articles of clothing so that others will not sit next to them. It is an unwritten behavioral rule in Canada and the United States not to sit next to someone if there is space somewhere else. You would be considered an intruder or an invader of other people's personal space if you sat next to them while there were other seats available. In fact, the person whom you sat next to might just get up and leave or stare at you angrily. These kinds of rules on the use of space vary significantly from one culture to another. Once in Palermo, where I was making the film mentioned earlier, five of us were taking a break and sitting in a circle on an almost deserted beach when suddenly an Italian family with many children came and sat next to us and started talking and laughing and playing. With all that space available this behavior seemed rather bizarre. We felt they were invading our privacy. When I asked our interpreter about this behavior, she said it was not at all uncommon in Sicily. People like to be near other people. They gravitate together rather than stay apart. In movie theaters in Sicily, strangers often sit next to each other when there are empty seats all around them.

At airports, people watching will help you pass the time while waiting for a flight. This is also fertile ground for people watching. Why give in to frustration and anxiety when you find that your flight has been delayed? Relieve the stress by watching how others deal with this all too common stressful situation. Do people argue with the airport personnel or sit and stew about the delay with an angry face, or do they seem to drift off into a state of suspended animation, faces blank, eyes glazed? If you want an uplift, go to the arrival gates and watch happy faces greeting each other with handshakes, kisses, and hugs. International arrival gates are even more interesting because you can see how people from other cultures greet each other. If you don't feel like walking around, try to guess what the various people in the lounge do for a living or where they are from.

Cafés are sanctuaries for people watching and, as I've indicated before, zoos and parks are especially good. Here people tend to drop their guard. Their behavior is more spontaneous. I've seen people mimic the monkey's facial expressions without even realizing they are doing it. Humans, of course, are great mimickers. We mimic each other continuously and sometimes begin to look and act like the people with whom we spend a great deal of time.

At the beach, people tend to relax and enjoy the surroundings. If you are in a strange city or country, all these places are good to visit. You feel less of a stranger because they are universal places of human interaction.

Think of some of the locations where you most enjoy people watching. What makes them appealing? What do you associate with these places? What are your preferred times for people watching? In our research we ask the subjects to rank order their favorite people-watching sites. Here are the results, from most to least popular:

1. work
2. anywhere, everywhere
3. subways
4. shopping malls
5. restaurants
6. streets
7. bars
8. any place where people wait
9. beaches, parks
10. airports
11. cars
12. stores
13. theaters

How-to-Watch Behavior:
SOFTNESS

Let's illustrate by going to a party. There are many things you can watch for within the framework of people watching as we have discussed it so far. Here are some especially relevant to the party situation. As the evening progresses, you can look at the *frequency* with which people touch each other, if at all. If you are at a Latin American or francophone Canadian party, you may notice that people touch each other more frequently and stand closer than at an American or anglophone Canadian party. You can also look at the *intensity* of facial expressions that may indicate excitement, interest, happiness, concern, or sadness. You can look at the *duration* of people's handshakes, eye contact, etc., and the *location* of physical contact (e.g., the wrist, shoulder, waist, etc.) And don't only notice others, do some self-watching. See how frequently, how long, where, and how intensely *you* touch people. It is good to be tuned in to how you react when certain things are done to you by different people in different situations. Putting yourself in the other's place is a way of developing empathy for and understanding of another person's feelings.

Other things you can focus on are *patterns* of behavior. Can you find someone exhibiting a set of behaviors (e.g., use of space, body orientation, gestures, and eye contact) that indicate an overall state of mind such as anxiety, abandon, ten-sion, or openness? See if the set of behaviors is demonstrating harmony, such as laughing or moving about the room in some kind of synchrony. (I have sometimes found myself caught up in other people's rhythms, when walking quickly or hurrying on the street, for instance.) Occasionally, nonverbal behavior or body language can be contagious and result in the synchrony and mirroring behavior mentioned earlier. Researchers have demonstrated that people who take on the facial expressions or emotions of others show similar physiological internal reactions; thus, at least for the moment, you may feel the happiness, joy, or sadness of another. *Posture sharing* of people locked in conversation can be striking to observe. People who are highly interested in or attracted to one another may gaze intently into each other's eyes and imitate each other's body posture and facial expressions without being aware of it.

How do we put this silent language to work for us and what role does "people relating" play? As should be clear by now, it is in the process of people watching that you begin to understand the nature and significance of nonverbal behavior. That understanding can be translated into guidelines for watching your own nonverbal behaviors more effectively.

In researching this book, I not only examined my own people-watching activities and surveyed those of others through the questionnaire, I also studied the literature on the subject with some care. One of my intentions through this process was to see if I could identify those kinds of nonverbal behaviors that contributed most to the establishment of rapport between people and which fostered satisfying and smooth conversations. I came up with eight behaviors that seemed to lead to that end. When the first letter of each is combined, the acronym SOFTNESS results.

Before presenting it, however, we must warn you that SOFTNESS is very monocultural. The practices described in it which can serve as guidelines for the individual in attempting to develop effective nonverbal behavior are those most commonly associated with Americans and anglophone Canadians. More on that in a moment.

SOFTNESS

Stance: Face the other person squarely and don't tilt back or away. At times, lean slightly forward, thus showing interest and involvement in what the other person is saying.

Open: Keep your arms at your sides and your body relaxed. This conveys that you are open to what the other person has to say. Avoid crossing your arms tightly over your chest, as it has the effect of raising a barrier between you and the other person and may give the impression that you are cold toward him or her.

Facial Expression: A positive, relaxed facial expression (especially a smile) makes the other person feel at ease and shows that you are interested in what she or he is saying. It also is contagious.

Touch: Caution! A handshake is common the world over, but be careful about more aggressive touching. Americans and Canadians tend to be rather ambiguous about it. Some people feel extremely uncomfortable when touched by a stranger in any way, though they will almost always participate in a handshake.

Nod: Head nods show that you understand what is being said and that you are listening.

Eye Contact: Fairly steady but not continuous eye contact is important, as it conveys that you are attentive to what is being said. Avoid staring.

Speech: Speak at a moderate pace, using *positive*, warm tones of voice.

Space: Interpersonal distance affects the degree of comfort people feel in social interaction. Arm's length is considered the most comfortable (or at least neutral) interpersonal distance for social conversations. An interpersonal distance that is too close may evoke anxiety, or one that is too far may communicate disinterest.

Let's do an exercise in interpersonal distance so you can

get a feel for how the SOFTNESS guidelines apply to you personally.

Interpersonal Distance

It will come as no surprise that people maintain more interpersonal distance between themselves and those with whom they feel uneasy, uncomfortable, or who pose a threat. For example, people maintain more distance from figures representing people from a different culture or race and from people who are in positions of authority (e.g., police, supervisors, or teachers) than from friends. Try the interpersonal distance test which follows. Imagine yourself interacting with each of the six different types of persons represented by the silhouettes below. The person on the left represents either your friend, a stranger, a drug addict, someone you admire, someone you dislike, or someone from a culture very different from your own. Draw a figure which will represent you and place yourself above one of the numbers.

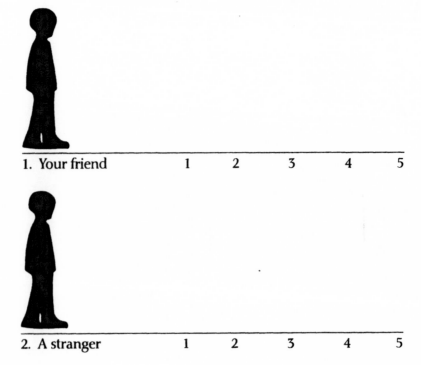

| 1. Your friend | 1 | 2 | 3 | 4 | 5 |

| 2. A stranger | 1 | 2 | 3 | 4 | 5 |

3. A drug addict   1   2   3   4   5

4. Someone you admire   1   2   3   4   5

5. Someone you dislike   1   2   3   4   5

6. Someone from a   1   2   3   4   5
very different culture

If you are like most of us you will no doubt feel closer to numbers 1 and 4; but further from numbers 2, 5, and 6; and very far from number 3. But this is only the beginning. Ponder the variations in your comfort distances. Have friends do the exercise and see if you can come up with different reactions. Do the exercise using other categories, e.g., people who are angry, sad, happy; who show you various gestures when you meet in different places; people in different positions of authority or who are well-known if not famous; or people who threaten you in different ways or to whom you pose a threat. Especially, identify real people in your life to assess in this manner.

How about a "space" expedition. Become an observer of the social distance you and others maintain in the course of daily life. Notice the space between people when in an elevator, waiting in line, conferring on the job, taking a break, dancing at a nightclub, walking into a sports arena, trying to get an autograph of a famous person, listening to a political speech. Note the effect of formality. In a courtroom, see how far the judge is kept from the defendant and the barriers that intervene.

As we noted above, SOFTNESS is monocultural. If you follow its guidelines, your nonverbal behavior will be relatively effective in the United States and anglophone Canada, but not necessarily in interactions with people from other cultures. Latins stand closer and Japanese further away, Indians (from India) nod agreement in a manner that appears to Americans to mean no, Africans and American blacks have different eye contact behaviors from European Americans, Japanese and Native Americans value silence in ways white Americans do not. We all know, therefore, that nonverbal behaviors vary, sometimes radically, from culture to culture. The question then becomes, how do we pursue our people-watching interests and develop guidelines for our own nonverbal behavior across cultures? That is the subject of the second part of this book.

PART II

People Watching across Cultures

Introduction

As was noted earlier, the observer who can recognize the range and meaning of nonverbal behavior has the opportunity to develop a deeper understanding of his or her immediate social environment. Such an individual also acquires a better cross–cultural appreciation of the human condition.

The study of intercultural communication, of which nonverbal behavior is a core dimension, has expanded rapidly in recent years but is still not widely understood. There is as yet little information available to the average person concerning how to comprehend nonverbal communication among people of different cultural backgrounds.

This second part of the book will attempt to improve the situation by discussing people watching across cultures. It will examine the general assumptions people make regarding the subject and list some of the variations in nonverbal communication among the cultures of the world. It will show that the failure to understand these differences can lead to the sending of confusing and conflicting messages and seriously disrupt communication. Further, it will draw attention to some of the more unfortunate results of making erroneous assumptions about the meaning of other people's nonverbal behavior and to the way people's perceptions of each other can be distorted.

Observing how people behave in public places can result in stereotypes, especially when the observer and observed are of different cultural backgrounds. Certain ethnic groups may be stereotyped (e.g., Italians or Israelis) as being too loud, too pushy, or too emotional by those (e.g., Anglo–Canadians) who tend to be more restrained or conservative in the use of their hands and in showing emotion. On the other hand, people who are more emotionally restrained can be stereotyped by those who are more emotionally expressive as being too cold or too distant. Stereotypes often develop from the nonverbal behaviors people use in public places because that is the behavior accessible for observation. For example, arguing, bargaining, or speaking loudly may be viewed as rude and inappropriate (e.g., in Anglo–Canada or among Americans of northern European descent). In some countries such as Hong Kong, Israel, Tunisia, and Mexico, it would be considered foolish not to bargain with the merchants. Even in English Canada it is possible to bargain with some merchants. I decided to test my bargaining skills in a very "proper" furniture store in downtown Toronto, Canada, on behalf of a student friend who needed some furniture. Surprisingly, I convinced the store manager to reduce a living room ensemble on sale for an additional 25 percent off a price already discounted by 15 percent. The store manager asked me if I would like a job selling furniture.

As mentioned earlier, vendors at markets are particularly interesting in their penchant for flamboyant behavior. Remember the vendor in Greece who became quite irritated when I picked up a tomato to feel it.

Finally, this part of the book will list some benefits of watching people from other cultures and will present a few exercises designed to develop your intercultural people-watching skills and understanding.

A Test of Assumptions about Nonverbal Behavior across Cultures

The following is a short exercise designed to illustrate the degree to which we accept dubious assumptions about the meaning of certain kinds of nonverbal communication. Is each of the short comments on the following pages true or false? Place a sheet of paper over the first statement and then slide it down just below the true or false question. When you have decided on the answer, circle it, and slide the paper down again to reveal the answer and compare it with yours. Continue on, answering each of the questions before looking at the answers. The answers were provided by people from the particular cultural groups being discussed; by professional psychologists, anthropologists, social scientists, and sociologists; and by researchers trained specifically in intercultural nonverbal behavior.

Ready? Turn the page and begin.

Test Your Assumptions about People from Other Cultures

1. Nonverbal communication is similar throughout all cultures.

   True or false?

   > *False.* Nonverbal communication can be culture-bound. Different cultures show marked differences in the physical distance they keep from other people, their use of certain facial expressions, body postures, eye contact, gestures, tone of voice, hesitations in speech, loudness of voice, and in many other nonverbal mannerisms.

2. People of all cultures show basic emotions through roughly the same facial expressions.

   True or false?

   > *True.* There is evidence of universal commonalities in facial expression which convey the basic emotions such as fear, happiness, and sadness.

3. Laughter is always a sign of happiness.

   True or false?

   > *False.* In some cultures, such as Japanese and Korean, laughter does not always mean that a person is happy. It sometimes means that he or she is embarrassed or anxious.

4. Masculinity among men is universally indicated by cool, logical, reserved behavior.

   True or false?

   > *False.* In Iran, for example, men are expected to be intuitive and to show their emotions. If they don't, and if they appear to be too logical, they are seen as being undependable and lacking a vital human trait.

5. A Brazilian man and woman, who are greeting or saying goodbye to each other, look into each other's eyes and exchange three kisses: A first kiss on the right cheek, a second on the left, and a third, again on the

right cheek. This indicates that they are sexually attracted to each other.

True or false?

False. Kissing as a greeting behavior between men and women is common among many people in Latin cultures. In Brazil, the exchange of three kisses is a common sign of friendliness.

6. A woman's blinking of her eyes at a man is a sign of coyness throughout the world.

True or false?

False. In Hong Kong, for example, blinking of the eyes at someone is considered impolite.

7. The discovery of a recessive gene which is carried by the majority of the people of Japan has documented the fact that the Japanese are biologically incapable of showing the full range of human emotions.

True or false?

False. A universal capability and similarity of expressions conveying the basic emotions has been demonstrated across cultures. Some cultures, however, may be perceived as being less demonstrative, while others (like the Japanese) restrain the public display of emotion.

8. A young West Indian who lowers his or her eyes while being harshly spoken to by an adult in authority is showing disrespect toward that person.

True or false?

False. In many Caribbean as well as West African and Latin countries, it is a sign of respect and submission for young people to lower their eyes when confronted by authority.

9. In Brazil, the "right-on" sign, made when forming a circle by touching the thumb and forefinger, is a rude gesture.

True or false?

> *True.* This sign, which in Brazil is usually
> made with the palm upwards, transmits a
> sexual or obscene meaning. (See my account
> of the incident in Brazil in chapter 3 (Part I) if
> you missed it!)

10. In England, a "V for Victory" sign, made with the palm
    of the hand facing the person doing the signaling, has
    for many centuries symbolized love.

    True or false?

    > *False.* In England, a "V for Victory" sign with
    > the palm of the hand facing the person doing
    > the signaling is an obscene gesture recorded
    > as early as 1913. Its popularity has waned in
    > the last few decades.

11. The "up yours" gesture, where the middle finger is
    jerked upwards at someone with whom one is an-
    noyed, has been in active use throughout many cul-
    tures and for over 2,000 years.

    True or false?

    > *True.* This gesture was known to the Romans,
    > who referred to the middle finger as the
    > impudent or obscene finger. Its use is also
    > recorded among Arabs, who often modify the
    > gesture by holding the hand, palm down,
    > with the offending finger pointing down-
    > ward.

12. An open hand thrust in the direction of a person's
    face means "halt" in all societies.

    True or false?

    > *False.* In Greece, this sign means "go to hell."

13. In Russia, receiving a super-slow handclap after a per-
    formance is a high compliment.

    True or false?

    > *True.* In Russia, this kind of applause signifies
    > great appreciation.

14. Tilting the head rhythmically from side-to-side means
    no in all cultures.

    True or false?

> *False.* In Bulgaria and parts of Greece, Yugo-
> slavia, Turkey, Iran, and Bengal, tilting the
> head from side to side, as in a pendulum arc,
> often means yes.

15. A Mexican businessman with whom you are beginning to have dealings invites you to meet him one
afternoon at 3:00 P.M. in his office. You arrive ten minutes early, only to find that he has not yet come back
from lunch. It is 3:45 P.M. before he calmly walks into
the office, without an apology for his lateness, and
introduces you to his brother who had joined him for
lunch. The businessman was trying to tell you that he
wasn't interested in doing business with you.

True or false?

> *False.* Not all cultures manage time in the
> same way. North Americans place a high
> value on time per se. They believe it should
> not be wasted. Adhering to schedules is one
> way they accomplish that. They therefore
> internalize their schedules (i.e., they are
> internally controlled by them). In other
> cultures, such as those of Latin America,
> schedules are of secondary importance.
> Attending to the needs and obligations of
> friends and relatives has a higher priority.
> The Mexican in this incident was simply
> following his own hierarchy of values.

16. In Latin countries, calling on someone and expecting
that person to rearrange his or her plans to suit you is
a way to express your caring or love for that person.

True or false?

> *True.* Latins, like people in a number of other
> cultures, stress the importance of commit-
> ment and obligation in their relationships
> with others. Expecting your friends to put
> themselves out for you shows how close they
> feel to you.

17. Americans are almost always perceived as loud, rude,
boastful, immature, disrespectful, and sometimes racist by the rest of the world.

True or false?

> *False.* Although this stereotype does exist, Americans are, in fact, perceived in different ways overseas, in many cases quite positively. They are not all "ugly Americans."

18. People tend to prefer those most like themselves in body language, dress, appearance, and values.

True or false?

> *True.* As a result of this, people tend to like, hire, and promote those who show similarity to themselves in these traits.

19. Actions speak louder than words.

True or false?

> *True.* Recently, a Brandeis University psychologist tested this idea and found that when there was a conflict between the way people described themselves and their actual behavior, those observing them usually gave more credence to behavior.

3

Cultural Myth and Cultural Context

Unfortunately, the view of those who are culturally or racially dissimilar is still colored by the essentially universal belief or assumption that one's own culture group and its ways are better than others. While most of us do not see ourselves as culturally biased, prejudiced, or racist, we do observe the world around us through our own cultural blinders and make judgments accordingly. What is right or normal is determined by what we learned growing up in our own society and is influenced by what the psychologist S. Keen refers to as our personal and cultural myths. These are the interlocking stories, rituals, rites, customs, and beliefs that convey a pivotal meaning and direction to a person, family, community, or culture; in other words, they are the underlying, unquestioned traditions and premises from which our lives and our culture get their impetus. Concepts such as the United States being the land of opportunity, special events such as one's senior prom or Bar Mitzvah, the story of Davy Crockett and that of the Alamo are all cultural myths, according to Keen, who draws a parallel between these myths and the "information" contained in the DNA of a cell or the disk of a computer. These myths serve as the cultural DNA, the software or the unconscious blueprint, which determines the way we see and relate to reality.

But these myths are not simply the conscious celebration of certain values, they are "an unconscious, habitual way of seeing things, an invisible stew of unquestioned assumptions." These assumptions, which lie for the most part beneath the surface of consciousness, are the foundation upon which we build our value system. Although they are hidden inside us, they shine through in our behavior so that outsiders are often able to perceive things about our basic beliefs that we ourselves cannot.

It is the assumptions that we accept and the myths by which we live that ultimately provide the context for our own nonverbal behavior. If some of the nonverbal behavior illustrated in the exercise at the beginning of this part seemed strange to you, it could have been because the behaviors were described without the cultural context which would have made them meaningful and normal to us. Birdwhistell, who has devoted his career to the study of human communication, has written that although everyone has the same range of physical movements, every person's actions must be considered within the context of the behavior, the place where it is occurring, the communication taking place, and the cultural influence on the individuals.

To understand better the importance of context, consider a Portuguese seeing an American tourist wearing jogging shorts, a cutoff T-shirt, and worn sneakers in the heart of downtown, fashion-conscious Lisbon. She or he might draw the conclusion that the visitor was sloppy and lacking in manners. Yet in the United States, jogging clothes and other casual dress are commonly seen and are an accepted part of the American social scene. One might find that the American is from a northerly climate and is simply taking advantage of the Portuguese sunshine. Or maybe we believe in the universality of "symbolic relations," as the academics like to call it. The Portuguese could assume that a relaxed style of dressing is a reflection of a de-emphasis on social status and that, since many Americans dress in this fashion, it signifies that class and status play a lesser role in their social environment than in that of some other cultures. Yet most tourists who are observed walking down the avenues of European cities do not stop to discuss their attitudes on clothing and its ramification on class structure with the local population. There really is no other way than that to decide what their opinions on the matter would be. The most obvious conclusion to be reached by our example is that some American tourists stand out in the streets of Lisbon by dressing more casually than the local population.

Thus we arrive at one of the fundamental principles of intercultural communication: that cultures are not usefully perceived as better or worse than one another, only as different. This is not to advocate cultural relativism, but by starting out observing differences in behavior nonjudgmentally, you are able to achieve some liberation from the cultural blinders that interfere with accurate perceptions across cultures. Seeing things in context helps, but context is more than just a setting for behavior. It is complex and dynamic and colors and directs behavior itself.

Edward T. Hall, a pioneer in the study of intercultural relations, suggests that societies can be distinguished by whether they are high context or low context. Low-context societies are characterized by a communication style which is logical, rational, and factual and which stresses the information to be transmitted; that is, a behavior or a communication is not dependent for much of its meaning on unstated social or cultural norms.

In a high-context society, on the other hand, the meaning of what is communicated depends heavily on the situation— who is communicating with whom under what circumstances and for what purpose, and so on. In high-context cultures, more is said with fewer words. By Hall's definition, Japanese society, with its emphasis on rank and hierarchy, face-saving and harmony, dependency and obligation, is high context, while the mainstream cultures of North America are literal, verbal, and explicit about the meaning of what is communicated—in short, low context.

There are also differences in the way cultures perceive time. Hall distinguishes between monochronic and polychronic cultures. People of monochronic cultures, such as northern Europeans and Anglo North Americans, schedule events as separate items—one at a time—in order to maintain an orderly succession in their lives and to minimize stress. This tends to lead them to internalize their schedule and, in a sense, they are controlled by it (recall the true/false question about the Mexican businessman on page 55). Those in polychronic cultures, on the other hand, are less time oriented. They don't compartmentalize their time as carefully. They are more casual about appointments and schedules. Being late is tolerated, or even expected, and they find themselves able to tend comfortably to more than one person or project at a time. They are, however, extremely involved with the business of regulating their human relationships. They have internalized, and are controlled by, the numerous obligations and duties toward those around them. Latin and Arab cultures, for example, are generally polychronic. You have probably heard such expressions as Mexican time or Brazilian time, which indicate the degree to which people in these cultures maintain flexibility in keeping appointments or arriving at parties. In Latin America, agreement to meet at 2:00 P.M. may only mean that it will be around 2:00 o'clock or, even, some time that afternoon, providing others don't interfere.

Consider how you feel when someone keeps you waiting or misses an appointment. Not only is it annoying, you are likely also to attribute to the person involved either negative character traits or deficient motivation or both—while, if you are dealing with someone from a polychronic culture, it may be simply that they are managing time differently from the way you manage it.

I remember once in Trinidad and Tobago, I had made arrangements to meet someone at a bar in Port of Spain at 8:00 P.M. When the clock struck 8:30 and my friend still hadn't arrived, I asked some Trinidadians who were sitting at the bar what I could expect. They told me to begin worrying only if 9:00 P.M. came around and the person still hadn't shown up. Sure enough, my friend arrived at 9:00, and we went on our way as if nothing had happened. In my own culture, if people come an hour late, there is no one there to greet them.

Recall my earlier discussion of proxemics, in which I noted that cultures have different ways of defining and using space. One of these is the notion of what constitutes a comfortable distance to maintain between people engaged in conversation (called "social distance"). Brazilians, for example, appear to position themselves closer to each other when interacting than do white Americans. Once, when advising a Brazilian woman, I deliberately sat closer to her than I normally do with advisees while conversing about a problem she was facing. She later told me that she had especially enjoyed talking to me on that occasion because I had sat closer to her than Anglo-Canadians normally do. This indicated to her that I was sincerely interested in her problem.

Hall describes how the Japanese prefer crowding in certain situations and how they have mastered the manipulation of space for artistic and aesthetic purposes. Space that Westerners would call empty is invested, by the Japanese, with meaning.

Differences in the use of space take many forms. North Americans appreciate homes with a lot of open space and wide, unfenced front yards. Latin Americans (and Australians) enclose their yards with high-walled fences. North Americans keep their doors open at the office, closing them only when an important meeting or activity requires privacy. Germans are more inclined to keep their doors closed and may see the openness of American offices as unbusinesslike.

As we have noted before, touching behavior varies widely among peoples and cultures. Latin or Mediterranean cultures are generally more contact-oriented than northern European or Asian cultures. In their everyday dealings with people, Latins and Arabs usually come closer, touch more, and use more expressive gestures than northern Europeans, North Americans, and Asians.

How do you feel when someone touches or stands or sits closer than the distance considered appropriate in your culture? Uncomfortable? Invaded or attacked? You are most likely from a noncontact culture imputing intention to someone from a contact culture.

Go to a public place like a shopping mall or restaurant and find a place where you can observe others inconspicuously. Count the number of times you see people touch others in a one-hour period. Note the sex and calculate the ages as well as the nationality of each pair. Try this exercise in an ethnic neighborhood, Chinese or Latino, for instance. Compare the results. Also, while traveling in other countries observe the touching behavior and the distance which people keep from each other in various settings.

Gestures are another type of nonverbal communication which show marked variation in meaning from culture to culture. Although gestures play a role in communication in all cultures, some (Mediterranean cultures, for example) are generally much richer in their gestural usage than others.

4

The Canadian Gestures Test

Here is a test of your skill in decoding some common hand gestures Anglo-Canadians use in social situations. Start with one and continue to fifteen. Put your answers in the boxes under the categories of answers provided on page 65. Look at the table on page 66 for the answers.

UNIVERSITY OF WINCHESTER
LIBRARY

Wolfgang Canadian Gestures Test

Categories of Answers

Gesture Number	Do you recognize this gesture? Yes or No?	What does this gesture mean to you?	Do you use this gesture yourself? Yes or No?	How often do you use this gesture? 1=rarely 5=often
1				
2				
3				
4				
5				
6				
7				
8				
9				
10				
11				
12				
13				
14				
15				

Answers and Performance of Culture Groups						
		% recognized (% correctly answered)				
Gesture	Meaning	Canadian		Asian		Mediterranean
		M F		M F		M F
1	A-OK	100 100 (100 100)		100 92 (100 100)		80 100 (90 100)
2	Be quiet	100 100 (100 100)		83 91 (100 100)		100 87 (90 100)
3	Yawn/tired/ bored	100 100 (100 100)		50 50 (67 100)		100 87 (90 100)
4	Up yours	100 100 (100 100)		67 8 (100 75)		30 72 (80 100)
5	How are you?	100 100 (100 100)		84 33 (100 100)		60 63 (90 100)
6	Can't hear you	100 100 (100 100)		100 100 (100 100)		70 75 (100 100)
7	Stop	100 94 (100 100)		100 75 (100 100)		80 100 (100 100)
8	Hi/Bye	100 100 (100 100)		84 100 (100 100)		80 100 (90 100)
9	Shrug/ Don't know	100 100 (100 100)		100 50 (100 100)		10 87 (90 100)
10	Thinking	100 100 (100 100)		100 66 (100 100)		90 100 (100 100)
11	Warn/scold	100 100 (100 100)		67 50 (100 92)		100 100 (100 100)
12	Beckon/ come here	100 100 (100 100)		83 92 (84 92)		100 100 (90 88)
13	What time is it?	100 100 (100 100)		84 42 (100 100)		100 100 (100 100)
14	Uncertain	100 100 (100 100)		67 50 (84 100)		100 100 (90 100)
15	Who me?	100 87 (100 87)		67 60 (84 67)		90 75 (90 100)

Compare yourself with the Canadians who took this quiz. As you can see in the table on p. 66, a high percentage of urban Anglo-Canadians recognized and accurately interpreted the gestures, as you would expect. American readers probably did too. If you are not North American, how familiar were you with the gestures? Do you use any of them yourself?

Since Canada is a multicultural country, a country of immigrants from different parts of the world, the gestures no doubt reflect its multicultural composition. When the test was given to some recent immigrants to Canada from Asia and the Mediterranean, a high percentage of the gestures used in Canada were already recognizable and accurately identified by them. Their scores are also indicated in the table.

If you want to take a survey of the common gestures used in your country or the area in which you live, a sample of some interview questions is provided on the next page so that you can generate your own gestures inventory. Answer the interview questions yourself first.

Interview Questions for Gestures Inventory

Birthplace:

Education:

Profession:

1. Describe some common hand gestures you use. In what situations do you use these gestures and to whom?

2. Describe which hand gestures you like to use. In what situations? What do they mean? Give some examples.

3. Describe which hand gestures you like to receive from others. In what situations? What do they mean? Give some examples.

4. Describe some hand gestures you dislike to give. What do they mean? Give some examples.

5. Describe which hand gestures you dislike to receive from others. What do they mean? Give some examples.

6. Are there any sounds you make to others to show how you are feeling (e.g., sound of frustration—suck the teeth; sound to get attention—psst, psst)? What do they mean?

7. Are there any hand gestures—other than those listed in 4 and 5 above—that you find obnoxious, vulgar, or impolite? In what situations are the gestures used? What do they mean? Give some examples.

5

Observing Gestures and Other Nonverbals across Cultures

The next time you are watching a foreign movie, observe what the characters are doing with their hands, face, head, and body. Note rude and unusual gestures and consider how they could be misunderstood in your country. Try sometime to discover what emotions two people in a café, especially one in another country, are conveying and what they are enjoying or not enjoying by observing only their gestures. If you are a teacher, observe the nonverbal behavior of students from other cultures in your class and compare it to those of the students from your own culture. Do you sometimes react negatively to behaviors which, in the cultural context of those students, may be perfectly acceptable? Further inquiry might enable you to teach these students more effectively. While watching a movie on television, turn off the sound. Can you tell what is going on by the actors' nonverbal behavior? Using a VCR will enable you to play back immediately and listen to the dialogue in a scene you have just watched without sound.

Eye contact and gazing behavior are also culturally influenced. For example, too much eye contact is seen as threatening by the Japanese. Similarly, blacks in the United States associate looking an authority figure directly in the eye with a lack of respect and perceive that this behavior has negative overtones. On the other hand, women of Tuareg, a North African culture, stare at each other relentlessly while talking—perhaps as a way to compensate for the limits to observing each other's facial expressions imposed by the wearing of veils which their culture requires.

North American women who travel to Latin countries are frequently unnerved by the tendency of Latin men to look them over from head to toe or to stare at them fixedly. Yet this action is accepted in most of these societies and is even seen as healthy masculine behavior. I was once told the story of a Portuguese man who had hosted one of his friends from Canada. This Portuguese wondered if the Canadian was not interested in women, since, in all of the trips they had taken together to the beaches and the various sights in Lisbon, the Canadian had never once looked at the man's lovely daughter, or at other women, in the head-to-toe fashion common in his culture.

There are also cultural differences in the timing of nonverbal activity. In school counseling and job interviews, for example, the timing involved in listening and speaking behavior was found by one researcher to be dissimilar between American whites and blacks. The speech patterns of white counselors contained a consistent and regular incidence of pauses and of breaking intonation combined with the expectation that the blacks would engage in appropriate listening behavior, such as nodding the head occasionally, looking the speaker more or less steadily in the eye, and muttering an "mm...hmm," from time to time. But black communication styles were found to be different from those of whites in the timing of their response patterns and in the length of eye contact. When the whites did not receive the expected signals, they tended to "speak down" to the black listeners and to ask them repeatedly if they understood as they overexplained and oversimplified their message.

In another case, a student of mine who had traveled to Portugal and who spoke Portuguese fluently described how in Lisbon he was frequently cut off in midsentence by those to whom he was speaking. He first considered it a mark of rudeness and ignorance, only to discover later that it was a sign of interest in him and in what he was talking about. Conversely, his methodical, North American "listen, stop-to-contemplate, then speak" conversational style came across to the Portuguese as a sign of disinterest, coldness, and sometimes evasion.

Attitudes toward tone and volume of voice vary too from culture to culture. In the Arab world, loudness is a sign of sincerity and warmth while, to Americans, this quality is often equated with aggression and is offensive (to many Asians it is the Americans who seem loud and aggressive). The next time you visit another country, go to a public square, especially a street market, close your eyes, and listen to how the volume of sound varies from that at home. (Or you can do this at an ethnic marketplace in your own country.) If there is a difference in the volume, how does it affect you?

There are even culturally influenced differences in attitudes toward body odors. For example, Arabs do not hesitate to breathe on people when they talk. It demonstrates friendship, since to deny one's breath to a friend is to be ashamed. Exchanging odors is a way Arabs involve themselves with each other. The Japanese, on the other hand, once regarded those men who possessed a strong underarm odor as having an illness and even accepted this malady as grounds for exclusion from military service.

Types of Nonverbal Behavior: An Outline

As you can see, people watching across cultures can be a complex and tricky business. Here is a guide to help you chart the process.

Types of Nonverbal Behavior

TOUCH

playful:	yes___ no___
hug:	yes___ no___
self-touch:	yes___ no___
body location:	mid___ upper___ lower___
duration:	short___ medium___ long___
strength:	light___ medium___ strong___
intention:	accidental___ intentional___

GREETINGS

handshake:	yes___ no___
smile:	yes___ no___
head nods:	yes___ no___
kiss on the cheek(s):	yes___ no___

raised eyebrows: yes___ no___

duration of greeting: _____

HAND GESTURES

expressive___ unexpressive___

positive___ negative___

accompanying speech: yes___ no___

GAZE

looks up___ looks down___

looks to side___ avoidance___

intense: yes___ no___

stare: yes___ no___

EYE CONTACT

yes___ no___

frequent___ infrequent___

FACIAL EXPRESSIONS

happy___ angry___

neutral___ sad____

surprise___ interest___

smile: relaxed___ forced___

attractiveness of face:

1	2	3	4	5
Low				High

STATURE

tall___ average___ short___

slim___ medium___ large___

attractiveness:

1	2	3	4	5
Low				High

DRESS
sloppy___ neat___
colorful___ dull___
business___ leisure___
traditional: yes___ no___
trendy:

1	2	3	4	5
Low				High

COORDINATION OF MOVEMENTS*
posture mirroring: yes___ no___
gesture mirroring: yes___ no___
similar facial expressions: yes___ no___
*similarity of movement and/or gestures of people interacting

INTERPERSONAL DISTANCE
near___ far___ intermediate___
comfortable: yes___ no___

POSTURE
leans forward___
leans backward___
open___ closed___
relaxed: yes___ no___

BODY ORIENTATION
toward___ away___
direct___ indirect___

WALKING STYLE
fast___ slow___
strides:
  long___ short___ medium___
  self-assured___ uncertain___
leisurely: yes___ no___

SMELL

    pleasant___ unpleasant___

    strong___ weak___

    type of odor/scent_____

SPEECH

    volume:

        loud___ soft___ medium___

    speed:

        fast___ slow___ medium___

    silent periods:

        frequent___ infrequent___

Developing Skills in Cross-Cultural People Watching

Cultural differences often create misunderstandings and conflict between those from different cultural backgrounds. In the workplace, contact–oriented workers may put off non-contact workers by standing too close or touching too often. People of the same nationality but of different race or culture, such as American whites and blacks, may misunderstand the meaning of one another's eye movements, body posture, and tone of voice. There may even be breakdowns at the level of entire communities. Hall, in his book *The Dance of Life: The Other Dimensions of Time* (1983), describes the friction between Native Americans and United States government agents, who viewed the former's lack of commitment to a schedule as wholesale community ingratitude for the projects which their reservations had been granted.

If you have a misunderstanding with someone from another culture, detach yourself for a moment from the situation and be the people watcher you are training yourself to become. Observe other aspects of the person's nonverbal repertoire to see if there is a congruence between what you think he or she is trying to convey to you and what you perceive is actually being conveyed.

There are other ways to improve your observational skills. The next time you get a phone call from someone whom you have never met, listen carefully to the voice and to the way of talking. Try to visualize his or her appearance (i.e., age, height, weight, hair color, facial features, etc.). Take quick notes on the pad next to your phone as soon as you have finished speaking. When you have done this, or later when you have more time, draw a quick sketch or word picture of the person, according to your notes and your memory of the conversation. When you finally meet the person, compare your notes and your sketch or word picture with the reality. Close? Utterly different? What does this tell you about your ability to generalize about and visualize people according to your preconceived notions of what the sound of a voice can convey? What does it tell you about your ability to draw conclusions about people from other cultures by observing only a single dimension of their behavior?

As I have emphasized before, ultimately myths, assumptions, and distorted conclusions create stereotypes. A stereotype is an exaggerated belief associated with a category of people. Its function is ultimately to justify our conduct in relation to those people. Because it is based on generalizations, a stereotype denies the potential for human individuality in all those that it encompasses. It also prevents us from really understanding the people we are observing. In a study of 140 corporate recruiters who were asked to choose—merely by reading their applications—between two men who were identically qualified except that one was 6'1" tall and the other 5'5", only 1 percent of the recruiters chose the shorter man (Knapp 1980). Obviously, shorter men are stereotyped as being less capable employees.

In an article "Self-fulfilling Stereotypes," M. Snyder relates the findings of experiments which suggested that in interracial encounters, racial stereotypes may constrain the participants to the extent that they cause them to act in accordance with these stereotypes irrespective of the real behavior they encounter. Snyder also remarks that even people who have developed doubts about the accuracy of their stereotypes probably proceed to test them by gathering the evidence that would appear to confirm them. Others have suggested that the nonverbal behaviors of those who are often subordinate to the dominant culture group in a society (women and minorities, for instance), often reflect the status which they occupy in that society. Tom in *Uncle Tom's Cabin* is an extreme case in point. The kind of obsequious behavior he displayed has long been unacceptable to blacks and currently to most whites as well.

In order to challenge your stereotypes and be a true cross–cultural people watcher, you must continually question your assumptions when you are observing those of other cultures. If you observe that a specific group of people talk too loudly, you must question what cultural norm constitutes "loud enough." If you perceive them to be distant, cold, and re–moved from you and from each other, you must come to terms with how you define "cold."

Beauty is in the eye of the beholder and is therefore deter–mined by cultural norms. Some cultures consider protruding buttocks as a sign of great beauty in a woman; others (in–cluding European society during the Renaissance) prefer plump rather than slim women. Sexy men may be tall, dark, and handsome, muscular and athletic, or suave and well–mannered. The important thing is trying not to impose your norms, prejudices and stereotypes on others. Appreciate the clothing, adornment, food, and music of other cultures for their inherent beauty. Who knows, you may discover a whole new way of perceiving beauty.

Differences in values and norms affect even basic impulses that should transcend culture. A kind word or act in any society should elicit a similar response, while harsh or dis–dainful treatment will create anger and resentment. The dif–ficulty lies in knowing what constitutes a kind act. A kind act in one culture may not necessarily be a kind act in another. A Japanese person may be highly offended and lose face by receiving an unexpected gift from a friend or neighbor on Christmas Eve when there is no opportunity to present a gift in return. In another example, the striking of children by their parents is seen by many Americans as child abuse, but the sending of a child to bed without supper for a gross misbe–havior is regarded as an act of discipline motivated by love and kindness. Yet most Portuguese would view the denial of food to their children as the ultimate sign of coldness and lack of love, while physical punishment is regarded by many as a sign of caring.

What are some of the concrete benefits of people watching across cultures? It will be valuable to the degree it sharpens your skills in observing and understanding nonverbal cues.

It has the potential also of enabling you to build rapport and trust with peoples from other cultures. For example, in one study English students from Oxford were trained to behave nonverbally like Arab students. As a result, the Arabs became more willing to share flats with them than with those who did not receive that training. If you are a member of a minority group, you may find your chances of being hired better if you learn the nonverbal behavior of those, assumably from the dominant culture, interviewing you for a job. For businesspersons, people watching may make you more sensitive to your clients from other cultures; and, if you become adroit enough at nonverbal communication to adapt your own nonverbal repertoire to suit that of your clients, you could become more effective in both expanding your business and dealing with people in general. Fiorello La Guardia, mayor of New York during the 1930s and 1940s, maintained the goodwill of three culture groups (Jews, Italians, and WASPS) by being fluent in the nonverbal communication of each. It was said that, in observing him give a speech, one could determine the group to which he was speaking simply by watching his body language.

It is clear that in the global village in which we live today, the kind of cross–cultural understanding and interaction skills needed will follow, at least in part, from the systematic pursuit of people watching and the mastery of nonverbal communication.

References

References

Allport, G. *The nature of prejudice.* 7th ed. Reading, MA: Addison-Wesley, 1954.

Archer, D. *How to expand your social intelligence quotient.* New York: M. Evans, 1980.

Argyle, M. *Bodily communication.* London: Methuen, 1975.

Argyle, M., A. Furnham, and J. A. Graham. *Social situations.* New York: Cambridge University Press, 1981.

Axtell, R. E. *Do's and taboos around the world.* New York: John Wiley, 1985.

———. *Gestures: The do's and taboos of body language around the world.* New York: John Wiley, 1991.

Bancroft, G. W. "Teacher education for the multicultural reality." In *Education of immigrant students: Issues and answers,* edited by A. Wolfgang. Toronto: Ontario Institute for Studies in Education, 1975.

Birdwhistell, R. *Kinesics and context.* Philadelphia: University of Pennsylvania Press, 1970.

Collett, P. "Training Englishmen in the nonverbal behaviour of Arabs." *International Journal of Psychology* 6, (1971): 209–15.

Cooper, K. *Nonverbal communication for business success.* New York: AMACOM, 1979.

Cousins, N. *Anatomy of an illness.* New York: Norton, 1979.

Csikszentmihalyi, M. *Flow: The psychology of optimal experience.* New York: Harper Perennial, 1990.

Davis, F. *Inside intuition.* New York: Signet, 1973.

Delmar, K. *Winning moves: The body language of selling.* New York: Warner Books, 1984.

Eibl-Eibesfeldt, I. "Universals in human expressive behavior." In *Nonverbal behavior: Applications and cultural implications,* edited by A. Wolfgang. New York: Academic Press, 1979.

Ekman, P., and W. V. Friesen. "Constants across cultures in the face and emotion." *Journal of Personality and Social Psychology* 17, (1979): 124–29.

Ekman, P., and H. Oster. "Facial expression of emotion." *Annual Review of Psychology* 30, (1979): 527–54.

Ekman, P., E. R. Sorenson, and W. V. Friesen. "Pan-cultural elements in facial displays of emotion." *Science* 164, (1969): 86–88.

Erikson, F. "Some cultural sources of miscommunication in interracial interviews." In *Nonverbal behavior: Perspectives, applications and intercultural insights,* edited by A. Wolfgang. Toronto: C. J. Hogrefe, 1984.

Galloway, C. M. "Nonverbal and teacher-student relationships: An intercultual perspective." In *Nonverbal behavior: Perspectives, applications and intercultural insights,* edited by A. Wolfgang. Toronto: C.J. Hogrefe, 1984.

Goffman, E. *Frame analysis.* New York: Harper and Row, 1974.

Hall, E. T. *The silent language.* New York: Doubleday, 1959.

———. *The hidden dimension.* New York: Doubleday, 1966.

———. *Beyond culture.* Garden City, NY: Doubleday, 1976.

———. *The dance of life: The other dimensions of time.* New York: Doubleday, 1983.

Hanna, J. L. "Black/white nonverbal differences, dance and dissonance: Implication for desegregation." In *Nonverbal behavior: Perspectives, applications and intercultual insights,* edited by A. Wolfgang. Toronto: C.J. Hogrefe, 1984.

Harper, R. G., A. N. Wieens, and J. D. Matarazzo. *Nonverbal communication: The state of the art.* New York: John Wiley, 1978.

Harrison, R. P. *Beyond words.* Englewood Cliffs, NJ: Prentice-Hall, 1974.

———. "Past problems and future directions in nonverbal behavior research: The case of the face." In *Nonverbal behavior: Perspectives, applications and intercultural insights*, edited by A. Wolfgang. Toronto: C. J. Hogrefe, 1984.

Henley, N., and M. La France. "Gender as culture: Difference and dominance in nonverbal behavior." In *Nonverbal behavior: Perspectives, applications and intercultural insights*, edited by A. Wolfgang. Lewiston, NY: C. J. Hogrefe, 1984.

Jones, J. M. *Prejudice and racism.* Reading, MA: Addison–Wesley, 1972.

Keen, S. "The stories we live by." *Psychology Today,* (December 1988): 43–47.

Kendon, A. "Did gesture have the happiness to escape the curse at the confusion of Babel?" In *Nonverbal behavior: Perspectives, applications and intercultural insights*, edited by A. Wolfgang. Lewiston, NY: C. J. Hogrefe, 1984.

Knapp, M. L. *Essentials of nonverbal communication.* New York: Holt, Rinehart and Winston, 1980.

Kohls, L. Robert. *Survival kit for overseas living.* rev. ed. Yarmouth, ME: Intercultural Press, 1995.

Kohn, A. "You know what they say…" *Psychology Today,* (April 1988): 36–41.

La France, M., and C. Mayo. "Cultural aspects of nonverbal communication: A review essay." *International Journal of Intercultural Relations,* (Spring, 1978): 71–89.

Language Research Centre. *Culturgrams: Hong Kong.* Provo, UT: Brigham Young University, 1980.

Leed, E. J. *The mind of the traveller: From Gilgamesh to global tourism.* New York: Basic Books, 1991.

Matternes, J. H. "The search for our ancestors." *National Geographic* 168, (October 1985): 560–623.

Mehrabian, A. *Silent messages: Implicit communication of emotion and attitudes.* Belmont, CA: Wadsworth, 1981.

Meltzoff, A. N., and M. K. Moore. "Imitation of facial and manual gestures by human neonates." *Science* 198, (1977): 75–78.

UNIVERSITY OF WORCESTER
LIBRARY

Montagu, A. *Touching: The human significance of the skin.* New York: Harper and Row, 1971.

Morris, D. *Manwatching: A field guide to human behavior.* New York: Harry Abrams, 1977.

———. *Bodywatching: A field guide to the human species.* London: Jonathan Cape, 1985.

Morris, D., P. Collect, P. March, and M. O'Shaugnessy. *Gestures.* New York: Stein and Day, 1979.

Peterson, R. T. *First guides: Birds of North America.* Boston: Houghton, Mifflin, 1986.

Ramsey, S. "Double vision: Nonverbal behavior east and west." In *Nonverbal behavior: Perspectives, applications and intercultural insights,* edited by A. Wolfgang. Lewiston, NY: C. J. Hogrefe, 1984.

Santoli, A. *Everything we had.* New York: Ballantine, 1981.

Smith, H. "Nonverbal behavioral aspects on teaching." In *Nonverbal behavior: Perspectives, applications and intercultural insights,* edited by A. Wolfgang. Lewiston, NY: C. J. Hogrefe, 1984.

Snyder, M. "Self-fulfilling stereotypes." *Psychology Today,* (July 1982): 60–68.

Sommer, R., and B. Sommer. *A practical guide to behavioral research.* New York: Oxford University Press, 1980.

Spradley, J. P. *The ethnographic interview.* Toronto: Holt, Rinehart and Winston, 1979.

———. *Participant observation.* Toronto: Holt, Rinehart and Winston, 1980.

Sussman, N. M., and H. M. Rosenfeld. "Influence of culture, language, and sex on conversational distance." *Journal of Personality and Social Psychology* 42, (1982): 66–74.

Vargas, M. F. *Louder Than words.* Ames: Iowa State University Press, 1986.

Visser, M. *The rituals of dinner.* Toronto: Harper Collins, 1991.

Von Raffler–Engel, W. "Nonverbal factor in minority interviewing." *Kinesis Report* 3, (1981): 15–18.

Vontress, C. E. Cross–cultural counseling: An existential approach. *Personnel and Guidance Journal* 58, (1979): 117–22.

Wolfgang, A., producer. *The Italian in transition*, (film). Toronto: International Tele-films Enterprises, 1973.

———. "Basic issues and plausible answers in counseling new Canadians." In *Education of immigrant students: Issues and answers*, edited by A. Wolfgang. Toronto: Ontario Institute for Studies in Education, 1975.

———. *The ABC's of expressing yourself with body language.* Toronto: Canadian Industry Resource Book, 1978.

———, ed. *Nonverbal behavior: Applications and cultural implications.* New York: Academic Press, 1979.

———. "Racial and ethnic minorities in the workplace: The importance of nonverbal communication." In *A resource book on racial and ethnic minorities in the workplace*, edited by T. Rees and L. Muszynski. Toronto: Social Planning Council of Metropolitan Toronto, 1982.

———. "The role and impact of nonverbal behavior in establishing and perceiving one's ethnic identity." In *Dominant national cultures and ethnic identities*, edited by J. Fijalkowski, H. Merkins, and F. Schmidt. Berlin: Freie Universität, June 1991.

———. *People watching at airports.* Toronto: Ontario Institute for Studies in Education, Department of Applied Psychology, 1991.

———. *People watching across cultures: Made easy.* Las Vegas: 2744 Quail Roost Way, Las Vegas, NV 89117, 1992.

———. *Nonverbal behavior: Perspectives, applications and intercultural insights.* 2d ed. Toronto: C. J. Hogrefe, 1995.

Wolfgang, A., and A. Bhardwahj. "One hundred years of nonverbal study." In *Nonverbal behavior: Perspectives, applications and intercultural insights*, edited by A. Wolfgang. Toronto: C. J. Hogrefe, 1984.

Wolfgang, A., and P. H. Waxer. "Training counsellors to enhance their sensitivity to nonverbal behaviour." In *Intercultural counselling and assessment*, edited by R. J. Samuda and A. Wolfgang. Lewiston, NY: C. J. Hogrefe, 1985.

Wolfgang, A., and M. Cohen. "Sensitivity of Canadians, Latin Americans, Ethiopians and Israelis to interracial facial expressions of emotion." *International Journal of Intercultural Relations* 12, (1988): 139–51.

Wolfgang, A., and Z. Wolofsky. "The ability of new Canadians to decode gestures by Canadians of Anglo-Celtic background." *International Journal of Intercultural Relations* 15, (1991): 47–61.

Zunin, L., and N. Zunin. *Contact: The first four minutes.* Los Angeles: Nash Publishing, 1972.

About the Author

Dr. Aaron Wolfgang is a licensed psychologist and a professor emeritus at the Ontario Institute for Studies in Education, which is affiliated with the University of Toronto. He was the founder and coordinator of the master's and doctorate focus in multicultural studies in the Department of Applied Psychology. He has edited two books on nonverbal behavior and organized two international conferences on the subject. His most recent book is entitled: *Nonverbal Behavior: Perspectives, Applications and Intercultural Insights.* He has produced two award–winning documentary films: *Body Language in the Classroom* and *The Italian in Transition.* Dr. Wolfgang teaches courses that deal extensively with techniques of observing people in general, including those from other cultures. To assess people's interpersonal sensitivity, he has created materials which examine perceptions of facial expressions and social distance and has recently developed a gestures test. Dr. Wolfgang helps train students and conducts workshops and seminars for business– and laypeople to be more observant and sensitive to nonverbal behavior. He was on the editorial board of the *Journal of Nonverbal Behavior* and has appeared on a variety of TV and radio shows.

Dr. Wolfgang has been a visiting scholar and has given seminars on nonverbal behavior at UCLA, University of the West Indies in Kingston and Trinidad and Tobago, University of Oxford, Bar–Ilan University in Israel, Max–Planck Institute of Human Etholgy in Germany, and Hokkai–Gakuen University of Kitami, Japan.

Born in Chelsea, Massachusetts, Aaron Wolfgang holds dual citizenship in the United States and Canada.

UNIVERSITY OF WINCHESTER
LIBRARY

Printed in the United Kingdom
by Lightning Source UK Ltd.
124231UK00001B/108/A